The Book of

RUTH

Start Publishing PD LLC

Manufactured in the United States of America

Cover art: Shutterstock/Taisiya Kozorez

Cover design: Jennifer Do

10 9 8 7 6 5 4 3 2 1

ISBN 979-8-8809-1087-8

The Book of

RUTH

CHAPTER 1

1:1 Now it came to pass in the days when the judges ruled, that there was a famine in the land. And a certain man of Bethlehemjudah went to sojourn in the country of Moab, he, and his wife, and his two sons. 1:2 And the name of the man [was] Elimelech, and the name of his wife Naomi, and the name of his two sons Mahlon and Chilion, Ephrathites of Bethlehemjudah. And they came into the country of Moab, and continued there. 1:3 And Elimelech Naomi's husband died; and she was left, and her two sons. 1:4 And they took them wives of the women of Moab; the name of the one [was] Orpah, and the name of the other Ruth: and they dwelled there about ten years. 1:5 And Mahlon and Chilion died also both of them; and the woman was left of her two sons and her husband. 1:6 Then she arose with her daughters in law, that she might return from the country of Moab: for she had heard in the country of Moab how that the LORD had visited his people in giving them bread. 1:7 Wherefore she went forth out of the place where she was, and her two daughters in law with her; and they went on the way to return unto the land of Judah. 1:8 And Naomi said unto her two daughters in law, Go, return each to her mother's house: the LORD deal kindly with you, as ye have dealt with the dead, and with me. 1:9 The LORD grant you that ye may find rest, each [of you] in the house of her husband. Then she kissed them; and they lifted up their voice, and wept. 1:10 And they said unto her, Surely we will return with thee unto thy people. 1:11 And Naomi said, Turn again, my daughters: why will ye go with me? [are] there yet [any more] sons in my womb, that they may be your husbands? 1:12 Turn again, my daughters, go [your way]; for I am too old to have an husband. If I should say, I have hope, [if] I should have an husband also to night, and should also bear sons; 1:13 Would ye tarry for them till they were grown? would ye stay for them from having husbands? nay, my daughters; for it grieveth me much for your sakes that the hand of the LORD is gone out against me. 1:14 And they lifted up their voice, and wept again: and Orpah kissed her mother in law; but Ruth clave unto her. 1:15 And she said, Behold, thy sister in law is gone back unto her people, and unto her gods: return thou after thy sister in

law. 1:16 And Ruth said, Intreat me not to leave thee, [or] to return from
following after thee: for whither thou goest, I will go; and where thou lodgest,
I will lodge: thy people [shall be] my people, and thy God my God: 1:17
Where thou diest, will I die, and there will I be buried: the LORD do so to
me, and more also, [if ought] but death part thee and me. 1:18 When she saw
that she was stedfastly minded to go with her, then she left speaking unto
her. 1:19 So they two went until they came to Bethlehem. And it came to
pass, when they were come to Bethlehem, that all the city was moved about
them, and they said, [Is] this Naomi? 1:20 And she said unto them, Call me
not Naomi, call me Mara: for the Almighty hath dealt very bitterly with me.
1:21 I went out full, and the LORD hath brought me home again empty: why
[then] call ye me Naomi, seeing the LORD hath testified against me, and the
Almighty hath afflicted me? 1:22 So Naomi returned, and Ruth the
Moabitess, her daughter in law, with her, which returned out of the country
of Moab: and they came to Bethlehem in the beginning of barley harvest.

CHAPTER 2

2:1 And Naomi had a kinsman of her husband's, a mighty man of wealth, o
the family of Elimelech; and his name [was] Boaz. 2:2 And Ruth the
Moabitess said unto Naomi, Let me now go to the field, and glean ears o
corn after [him] in whose sight I shall find grace. And she said unto her, Go
my daughter. 2:3 And she went, and came, and gleaned in the field after the
reapers: and her hap was to light on a part of the field [belonging] unto Boaz
who [was] of the kindred of Elimelech. 2:4 And, behold, Boaz came from
Bethlehem, and said unto the reapers, The LORD [be] with you. And the
answered him, The LORD bless thee. 2:5 Then said Boaz unto his servan
that was set over the reapers, Whose damsel [is] this? 2:6 And the servant tha
was set over the reapers answered and said, It [is] the Moabitish damsel tha
came back with Naomi out of the country of Moab: 2:7 And she said, I pra
you, let me glean and gather after the reapers among the sheaves: so sh
came, and hath continued even from the morning until now, that she tarrie
a little in the house. 2:8 Then said Boaz unto Ruth, Hearest thou not, m

daughter? Go not to glean in another field, neither go from hence, but abide here fast by my maidens: 2:9 [Let] thine eyes [be] on the field that they do reap, and go thou after them: have I not charged the young men that they shall not touch thee? and when thou art athirst, go unto the vessels, and drink of [that] which the young men have drawn. 2:10 Then she fell on her face, and bowed herself to the ground, and said unto him, Why have I found grace in thine eyes, that thou shouldest take knowledge of me, seeing I [am] a stranger? 2:11 And Boaz answered and said unto her, It hath fully been shewed me, all that thou hast done unto thy mother in law since the death of thine husband: and [how] thou hast left thy father and thy mother, and the land of thy nativity, and art come unto a people which thou knewest not heretofore. 2:12 The LORD recompense thy work, and a full reward be given thee of the LORD God of Israel, under whose wings thou art come to trust. 2:13 Then she said, Let me find favour in thy sight, my lord; for that thou hast comforted me, and for that thou hast spoken friendly unto thine handmaid, though I be not like unto one of thine handmaidens. 2:14 And Boaz said unto her, At mealtime come thou hither, and eat of the bread, and dip thy morsel in the vinegar. And she sat beside the reapers: and he reached her parched [corn], and she did eat, and was sufficed, and left. 2:15 And when she was risen up to glean, Boaz commanded his young men, saying, Let her glean even among the sheaves, and reproach her not: 2:16 And let fall also [some] of the handfuls of purpose for her, and leave [them], that she may glean [them], and rebuke her not. 2:17 So she gleaned in the field until even, and beat out that she had gleaned: and it was about an ephah of barley. 2:18 And she took [it] up, and went into the city: and her mother in law saw what she had gleaned: and she brought forth, and gave to her that she had reserved after she was sufficed. 2:19 And her mother in law said unto her, Where hast thou gleaned to day? and where wroughtest thou? blessed be he that did take knowledge of thee. And she shewed her mother in law with whom she had wrought, and said, The man's name with whom I wrought to day [is] Boaz. 2:20 And Naomi said unto her daughter in law, Blessed [be] he of the LORD, who hath not left off his kindness to the living and to the dead. And

Naomi said unto her, The man [is] near of kin unto us, one of our next kinsmen. 2:21 And Ruth the Moabitess said, He said unto me also, Thou shalt keep fast by my young men, until they have ended all my harvest. 2:22 And Naomi said unto Ruth her daughter in law, [It is] good, my daughter, that thou go out with his maidens, that they meet thee not in any other field. 2:23 So she kept fast by the maidens of Boaz to glean unto the end of barley harvest and of wheat harvest; and dwelt with her mother in law.

CHAPTER 3

3:1 Then Naomi her mother in law said unto her, My daughter, shall I not seek rest for thee, that it may be well with thee? 3:2 And now [is] not Boaz of our kindred, with whose maidens thou wast? Behold, he winnoweth barley to night in the threshingfloor. 3:3 Wash thyself therefore, and anoint thee, and put thy raiment upon thee, and get thee down to the floor: [but] make not thyself known unto the man, until he shall have done eating and drinking. 3:4 And it shall be, when he lieth down, that thou shalt mark the place where he shall lie, and thou shalt go in, and uncover his feet, and lay thee down; and he will tell thee what thou shalt do. 3:5 And she said unto her, All that thou sayest unto me I will do. 3:6 And she went down unto the floor, and did according to all that her mother in law bade her. 3:7 And when Boaz had eaten and drunk, and his heart was merry, he went to lie down at the end of the heap of corn: and she came softly, and uncovered his feet, and laid her down. 3:8 And it came to pass at midnight, that the man was afraid, and turned himself: and, behold, a woman lay at his feet. 3:9 And he said, Who [art] thou? And she answered, I [am] Ruth thine handmaid: spread therefore thy skirt over thine handmaid; for thou [art] a near kinsman. 3:10 And he said, Blessed [be] thou of the LORD, my daughter: [for] thou hast shewed more kindness in the latter end than at the beginning, inasmuch as thou followedst not young men, whether poor or rich. 3:11 And now, my daughter, fear not; I will do to thee all that thou requirest: for all the city of my people doth know that thou [art] a virtuous woman. 3:12 And now it is true that I [am thy] near kinsman: howbeit there is a kinsman nearer than I

3:13 Tarry this night, and it shall be in the morning, [that] if he will perform unto thee the part of a kinsman, well; let him do the kinsman's part: but if he will not do the part of a kinsman to thee, then will I do the part of a kinsman to thee, [as] the LORD liveth: lie down until the morning. 3:14 And she lay at his feet until the morning: and she rose up before one could know another. And he said, Let it not be known that a woman came into the floor. 3:15 Also he said, Bring the vail that [thou hast] upon thee, and hold it. And when she held it, he measured six [measures] of barley, and laid [it] on her: and she went into the city. 3:16 And when she came to her mother in law, she said, Who [art] thou, my daughter? And she told her all that the man had done to her. 3:17 And she said, These six [measures] of barley gave he me; for he said to me, Go not empty unto thy mother in law. 3:18 Then said she, Sit still, my daughter, until thou know how the matter will fall: for the man will not be in rest, until he have finished the thing this day.

CHAPTER 4

4:1 Then went Boaz up to the gate, and sat him down there: and, behold, the kinsman of whom Boaz spake came by; unto whom he said, Ho, such a one! turn aside, sit down here. And he turned aside, and sat down. 4:2 And he took ten men of the elders of the city, and said, Sit ye down here. And they sat down. 4:3 And he said unto the kinsman, Naomi, that is come again out of the country of Moab, selleth a parcel of land, which [was] our brother Elimelech's: 4:4 And I thought to advertise thee, saying, Buy [it] before the inhabitants, and before the elders of my people. If thou wilt redeem [it], redeem [it]: but if thou wilt not redeem [it, then] tell me, that I may know: for [there is] none to redeem [it] beside thee; and I [am] after thee. And he said, I will redeem [it]. 4:5 Then said Boaz, What day thou buyest the field of the hand of Naomi, thou must buy [it] also of Ruth the Moabitess, the wife of the dead, to raise up the name of the dead upon his inheritance. 4:6 And the kinsman said, I cannot redeem [it] for myself, lest I mar mine own inheritance: redeem thou my right to thyself; for I cannot redeem [it]. 4:7 Now this [was the manner] in former time in Israel concerning redeeming and concerning changing, for to confirm all things; a man plucked off his shoe, and gave [it] to his neighbour: and this [was] a testimony in Israel. 4:8 Therefore the kinsman said unto Boaz, Buy [it] for thee. So he drew off his shoe. 4:9 And Boaz said unto the elders, and [unto] all the people, Ye [are] witnesses this day, that I have bought all that [was] Elimelech's, and all that [was] Chilion's and Mahlon's, of the hand of Naomi. 4:10 Moreover Ruth the Moabitess, the wife of Mahlon, have I purchased to be my wife, to raise up the name of the dead upon his inheritance, that the name of the dead be not cut off from among his brethren, and from the gate of his place: ye [are] witnesses this day. 4:11 And all the people that [were] in the gate, and the elders, said, [We are] witnesses. The LORD make the woman that is come into thine house like Rachel and like Leah, which two did build the house of Israel: and do thou worthily in Ephratah, and be famous in Bethlehem: 4:12 And let thy house be like the house of Pharez, whom Tamar bare unto Judah, of the seed which the LORD shall give thee of this young woman. 4:13 So Boaz took Ruth, and she was his wife: and when he went in unto her, the LORD gave her conception, and she bare a son. 4:14 And the women said unto Naomi, Blessed [be] the LORD, which hath not left thee this day without a kinsman, that his name may be famous in Israel. 4:15 And he shall be unto thee a restorer of [thy] life, and a nourisher of thine old age: for thy daughter in law, which loveth thee, which is better to thee than seven sons, hath born him. 4:16 And Naomi took the child, and laid it in her bosom, and became nurse unto it. 4:17 And the women her neighbours gave it a name, saying, There is a son born to Naomi; and they called his name Obed: he [is] the father of Jesse, the father of David. 4:18 Now these [are] the generations of Pharez: Pharez begat Hezron, 4:19 And Hezron begat Ram, and Ram begat Amminadab, 4:20 And Amminadab begat Nahshon, and Nahshon begat Salmon, 4:21 And Salmon begat Boaz, and Boaz begat Obed, 4:22 And Obed begat Jesse, and Jesse begat David.

Other books in this series available from Sublime Books.

The Old Testament

978-1-5154-4078-9 The First Book of Moses: Genesis
978-1-5154-4079-6 The Second Book of Moses: Exodus
978-1-5154-4080-2 L The Third Book of Moses: Leviticus
978-1-5154-4081-9 The Fourth Book of Moses: Numbers
978-1-5154-4082-6 The Fifth Book of Moses: Deuteronomy
978-1-5154-4083-3 The Book of Joshua
978-1-5154-4084-0 The Book of Judges
978-1-5154-4085-7 The Book of Ruth
978-1-5154-4086-4 The First Book of Samuel
978-1-5154-4087-1 The Second Book of Samuel
978-1-5154-4088-8 The First Book of the Kings
978-1-5154-4089-5 The Second Book of the Kings
978-1-5154-4090-1 The First Book of the Chronicles
978-1-5154-4091-8 The Second Book of the Chronicles
978-1-5154-4092-5 The Book of Ezra
978-1-5154-4093-2 The Book of Nehemiah
978-1-5154-4094-9 The Book of Esther
978-1-5154-4095-6 The Book of Job
978-1-5154-4096-3 The Book of Psalms
978-1-5154-4097-0 The Proverbs
978-1-5154-4098-7 The Book of Ecclesiastes
978-1-5154-4099-4 The Song of Solomon
978-1-5154-4100-7 The Book of the Prophet Isaiah
978-1-5154-4101-4 The Book of the Prophet Jeremiah
978-1-5154-4102-1 The Lamentations of Jeremiah
978-1-5154-4103-8 The Book of the Prophet Ezekiel
978-1-5154-4104-5 The Book of Daniel
978-1-5154-4105-2 The Book of Hosea
978-1-5154-4106-9 The Book of Joel
78-1-5154-4107-6 The Book of Amos
78-1-5154-4108-3 The Book of Obadiah
78-1-5154-4109-0 The Book of Jonah

The Book of

978-1-5154-4110-6 The Book of Micah
978-1-5154-4111-3 The Book of Nahum
978-1-5154-4112-0 The Book of Habakkuk
978-1-5154-4113-7 The Book of Zephaniah
978-1-5154-4114-4 The Book of Haggai
978-1-5154-4115-1 The Book of Zechariah
978-1-5154-4116-8 The Book of Malachi

The New Testament

978-1-5154-4117-5 The Gospel According to Saint Matthew
978-1-5154-4118-2 The Gospel According to Saint Mark
978-1-5154-4119-9 The Gospel According to Saint Luke
978-1-5154-4120-5 The Gospel According to Saint John
978-1-5154-4121-2 The Acts of the Apostles
978-1-5154-4122-9 The Epistle of Paul the Apostle to the Romans
978-1-5154-4123-6 The First Epistle of Paul the Apostle to the Corinthians
978-1-5154-4124-3 The Second Epistle of Paul the Apostle to the Corinthians
978-1-5154-4125-0 The Epistle of Paul the Apostle to the Galatians
978-1-5154-4126-7 The Epistle of Paul the Apostle to the Ephesians
978-1-5154-4127-4 The Epistle of Paul the Apostle to the Philippians
978-1-5154-4128-1 The Epistle of Paul the Apostle to the Colossians
978-1-5154-4129-8 The First Epistle of Paul the Apostle to the Thessalonians
978-1-5154-4130-4 The Second Epistle of Paul the Apostle to the Thessalonians
978-1-5154-4131-1 The First Epistle of Paul the Apostle to Timothy
978-1-5154-4132-8 The Second Epistle of Paul the Apostle to Timothy
978-1-5154-4133-5 The Epistle of Paul the Apostle to Titus
978-1-5154-4134-2 The Epistle of Paul the Apostle to Philemon
978-1-5154-4135-9 The Epistle of Paul the Apostle to the Hebrews
978-1-5154-4136-6 The General Epistle of James

978-1-5154-4137-3 The First Epistle General of Peter
978-1-5154-4138-0 The Second General Epistle of Peter
978-1-5154-4139-7 The First Epistle General of John
978-1-5154-4140-3 The Second Epistle General of John
978-1-5154-4141-0 The Third Epistle General of John
978-1-5154-4142-7 The General Epistle of Jude
978-1-5154-4143-4 The Revelation of Saint John the Devine

www.ingramcontent.com/pod-product-compliance
Lightning Source LLC
Chambersburg PA
CBHW031956040826
48979CB00041B/446

* 9 7 9 8 8 8 0 9 1 0 8 7 8 *